2.B.A. MASTER

Arranged by John Nicholas

Pokémon 2.B.A. Master is available from Koch Records on CD (KOC8901-2 and KOC8902-2) and
Cassette (KOC8901-4 and KOC8902-4)

ISBN 978-1-57560-289-9

Visit our website at www.cherrylane.com

CONTENTS

Full-color pullouts follow page 16

Pokémon Theme

Words and Music by
T. Loeffler and J. Siegler

Moderately fast, with a driving beat

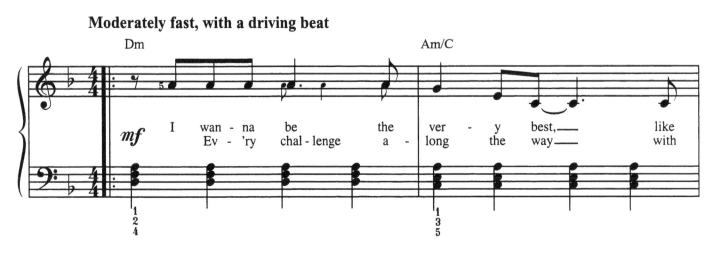

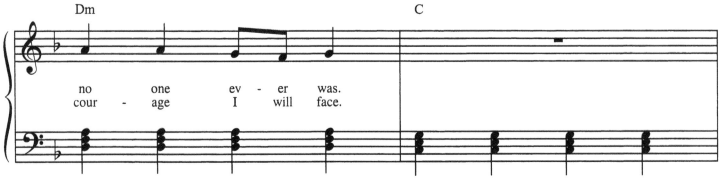

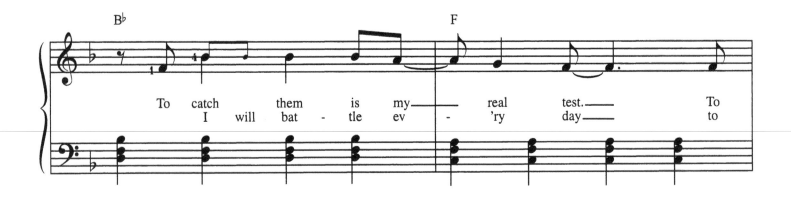

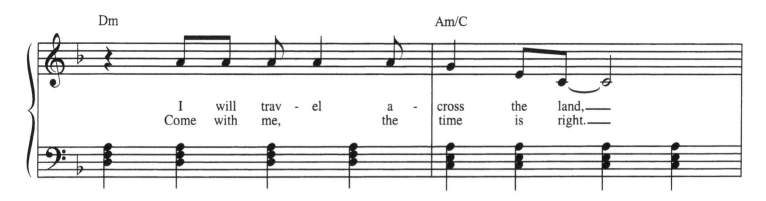

I will trav - el a - cross the land,____
Come with me, the time is right.____

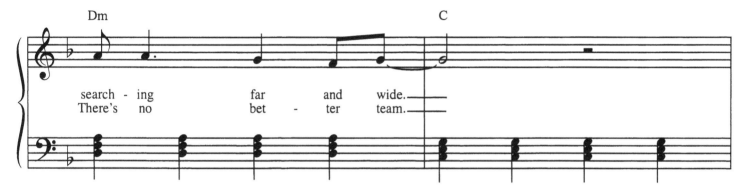

search - ing far and wide.____
There's no bet - ter team.____

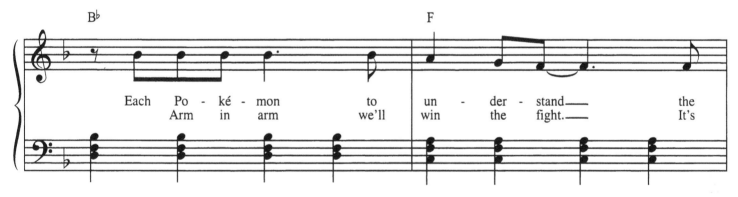

Each Po - ké - mon to un - der - stand____ the
Arm in arm we'll win the fight.____ It's

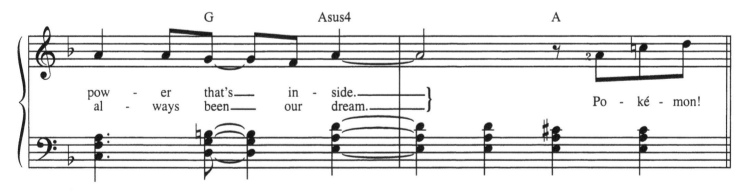

pow - er that's____ in - side.____
al - ways been____ our dream.____ Po - ké - mon!

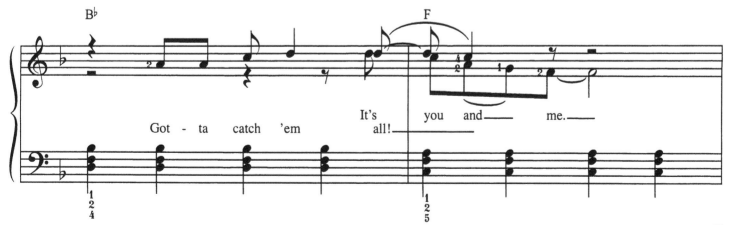

Got - ta catch 'em all!
It's you and____ me.____

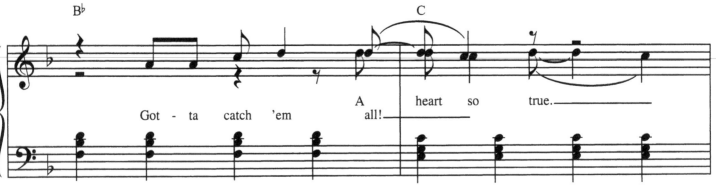

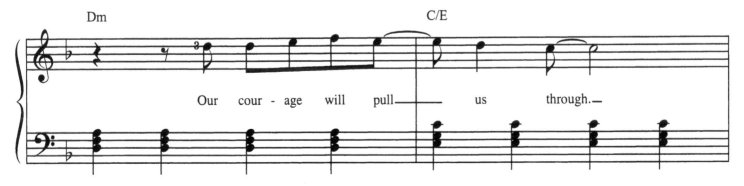

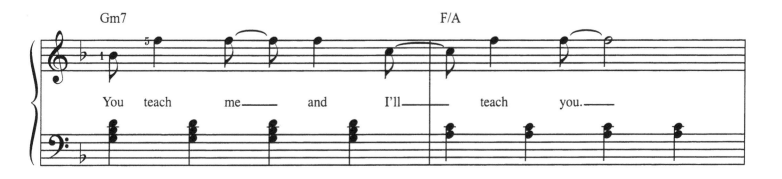

You teach me_____ and I'll_____ teach you._____

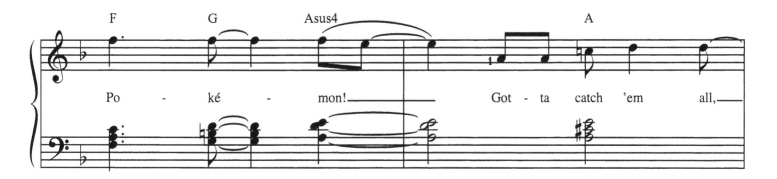

Po - ké - mon!_____ Got - ta catch 'em all,_____

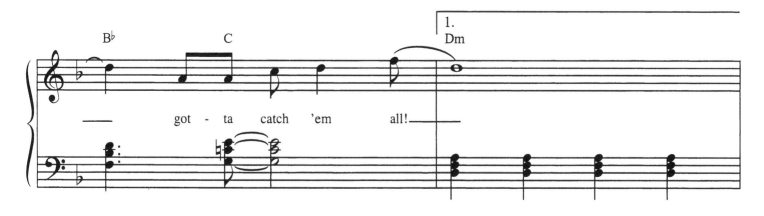

_____ got - ta catch 'em all!_____

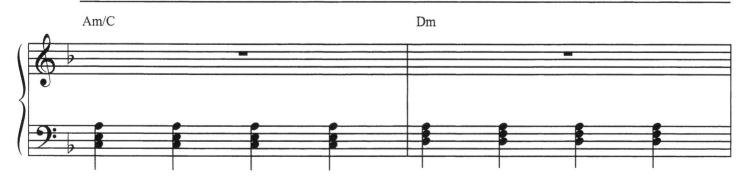

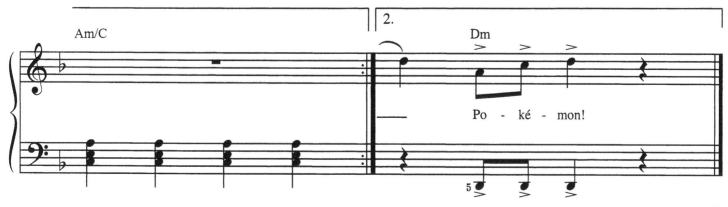

_____ Po - ké - mon!

2B A Master

Words and Music by
T. Loeffler and Russell Velazquez

Moderately, in 2

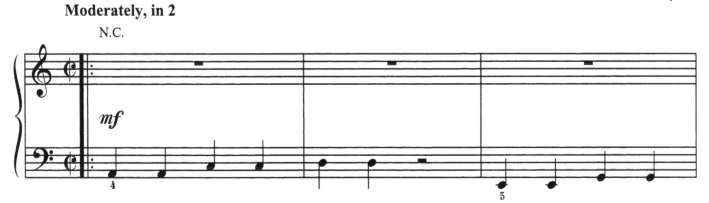

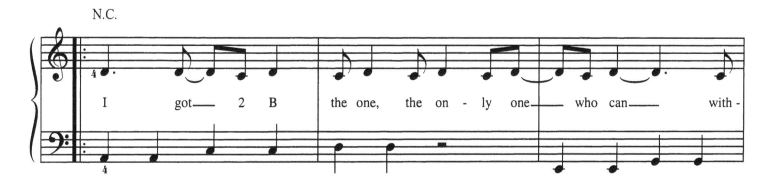

N.C.

I got 2 B the one, the on - ly one who can with -

stand the test 'n' B the best 'n' I got 2 strive, keep up

the drive, B a Mas - ter.

It takes a cer - tain kind of skill, and I won't stop un - til one

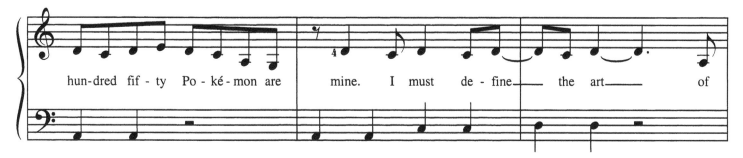

hun - dred fif - ty Po - ké - mon are mine. I must de - fine the art of

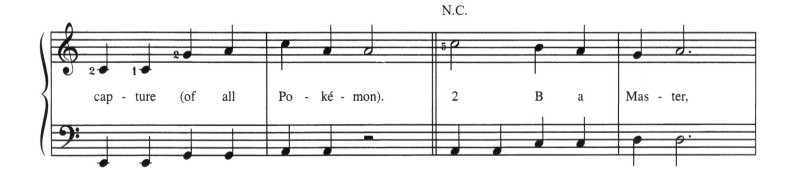

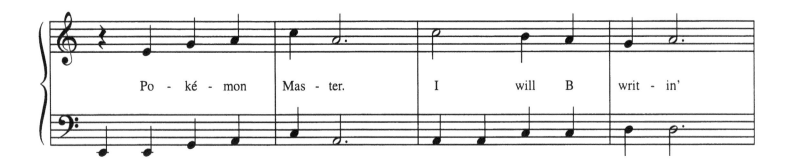

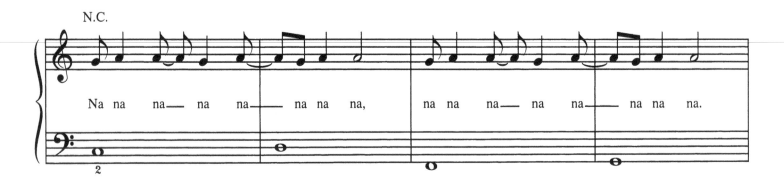

10

Na na na — na na — na na na, na na na — na na —

A7#9

N.C.

— na na. Po - ké - Ball. Go, go! Got my

badg — es and my Po - ké - Ball. Got my bud - dy Pi - ka -

chu 2 help me try 2 catch 'em all.

N.C.

Play 4 times

Rap (see additional lyrics)

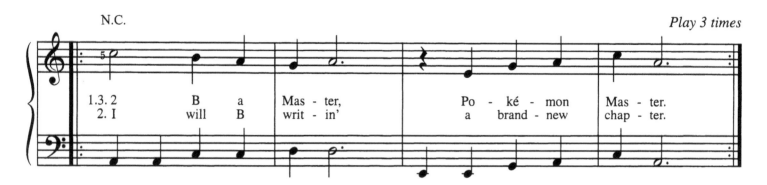

Play 3 times

1.3. 2   B   a   Mas - ter,   Po - ké - mon   Mas - ter.
2. I   will   B   writ - in'   a   brand - new   chap - ter.

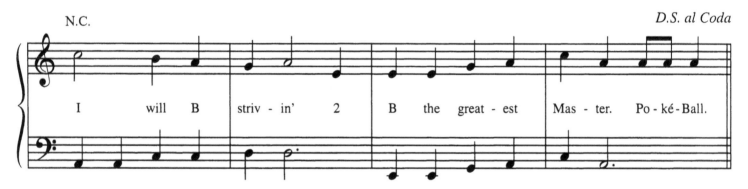

D.S. al Coda

I   will   B   striv - in'   2   B   the   great - est   Mas - ter.   Po - ké - Ball.

Coda

Na   na   na — na   na — na   na   na,   na   na   na — na   na —

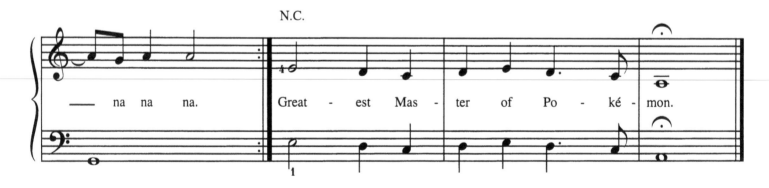

— na   na   na.   Great - est   Mas - ter   of   Po - ké - mon.

Rap:
Yo, it's all about the evolution of the Pokémon.
The training, attaining 'n' bein' part of the phenomenon.
B a Poké master icon. Ha!
Team Rocket will B long gone.
But first U gotta know about the different types:
Grass, Fire, Ground, Flame, Electric,
Water, Rock, Flying, Ice, Normal, Bug,
Ghost, Fighting & Dragon.
Don't forget about Psychic!

Viridian City

Words and Music by
T. Loeffler and Neil Jason

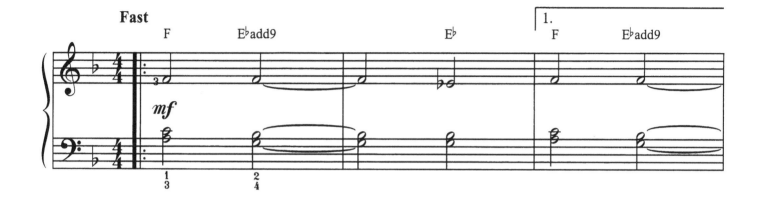

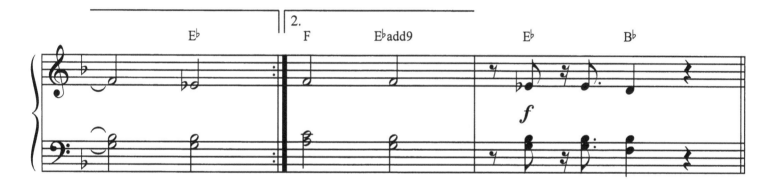

On the road to Vi - rid - i - an Cit - y.____

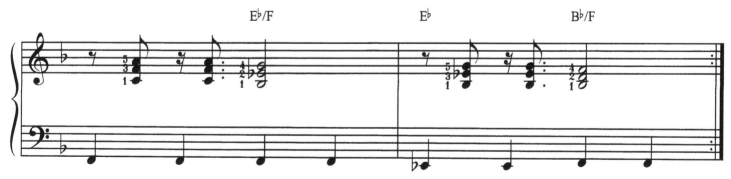

We've built a team and we've been train-
I left my home and now I see

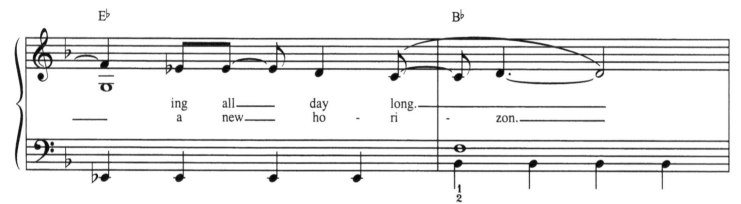

-ing all day long.
a new ho - ri - zon.

We're on the road and get-ting strong.
One day I'll come back to Pal-let town.

Now here's the plan: we're gon-na head
I'm on the road to be - come

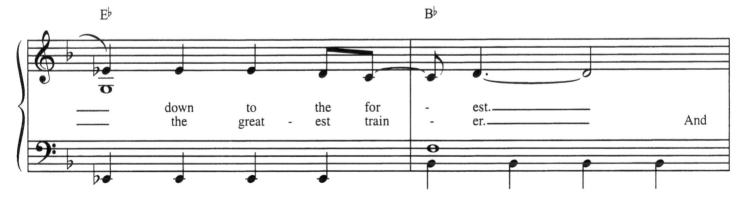

down to the for - est.
the great - est for train - er. And

14

F   E♭

Time to col - lect ____ some Po - ké - mon. ____
I won't quit un - til ____ I'm num - ber one. ____

B♭   Dm

We keep on try - in' ____ and then ____

C   B♭

____ we try some more ____ to stay to - geth - er and find a place ____

B♭/C

____ worth fight - ing for. ____ Oh, ____ I'm on the road. ____

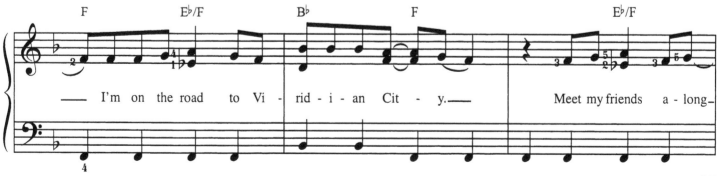

F   E♭/F   B♭   F   E♭/F

____ I'm on the road to Vi - rid - i - an Cit - y. ____ Meet my friends a - long ____

15

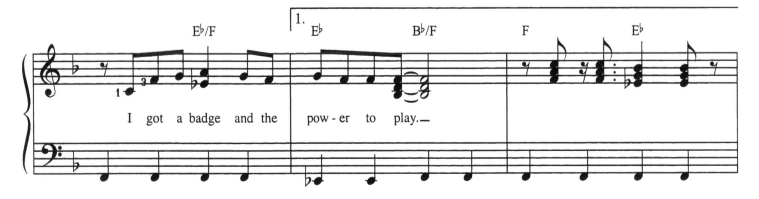

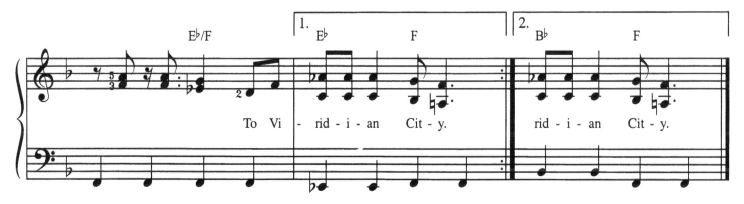

What Kind of Pokémon Are You?

Words and Music by
T. Loeffler, J. Siegler,
and Norman Grossfeld

Moderately, in 2

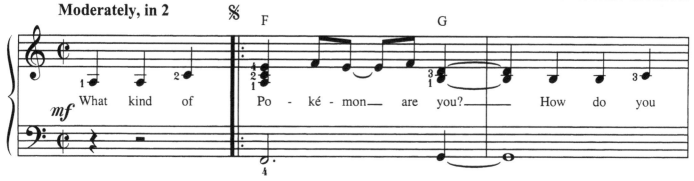

What kind of Po - ké - mon — are you? — How do you

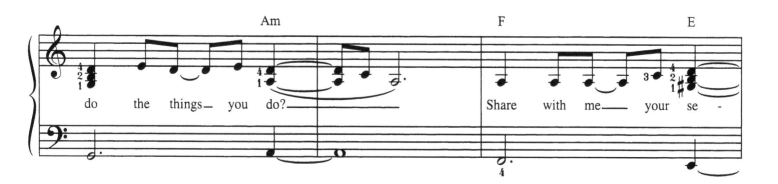

do the things — you do? — Share with me — your se -

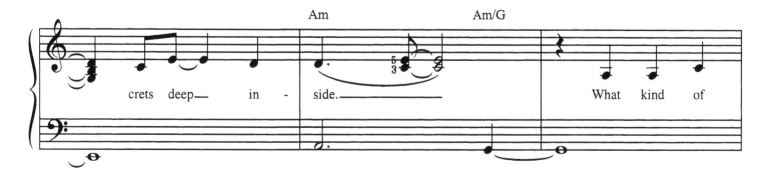

crets deep — in - side. — What kind of

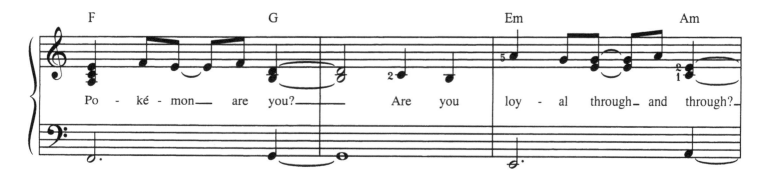

Po - ké - mon — are you? — Are you loy - al through — and through?

And do you have a heart that's___ true?___

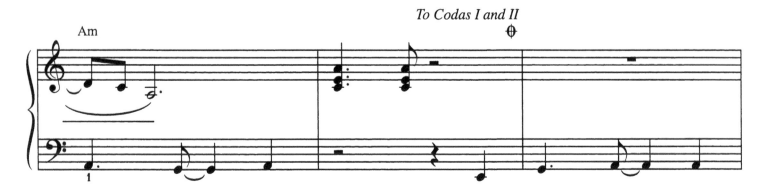

What kind of Po - ké - mon___ are you?___

To Codas I and II

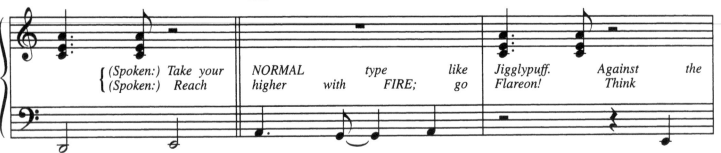

(Spoken:) Take your NORMAL type like Jigglypuff. Against the
(Spoken:) Reach higher with type FIRE; go Flareon! Think the

GHOSTLY Gengar, the battle's real tough. Thunderbolt's a great
twice about ICE to be number one. WATER'S in order if you

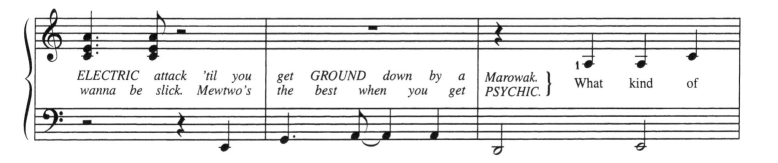

ELECTRIC attack 'til you | get GROUND down by a | Marowak. } What kind of
wanna be slick. Mewtwo's | the best when you get | PSYCHIC.

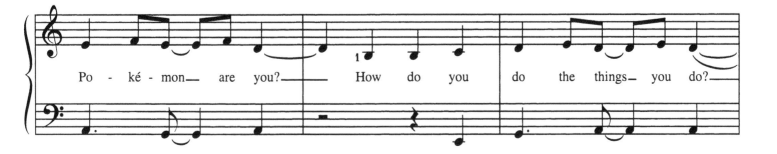

Po - ké - mon— are you?—— How do you | do the things— you do?——

{ Don't ya | BUG me with a | Caterpie. For a
{ Hitmonlee's | the key for your | FIGHTING mood and you can

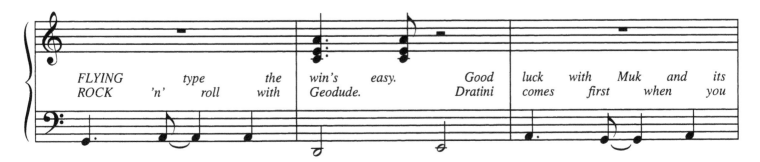

FLYING type the | win's easy. Good | luck with Muk and its
ROCK 'n' roll with | Geodude. Dratini | comes first when its

1.
N.C.

POISON gas. Make | one wrong move and it'll | kick your GRASS.
choose DRAGON, but | | What kind of

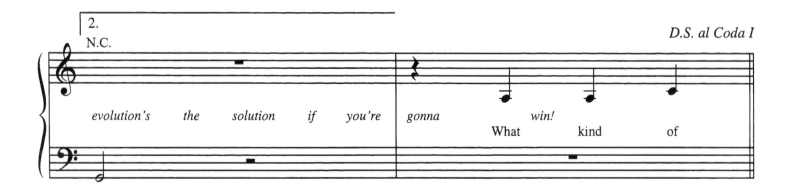

evolution's   the   solution   if   you're   gonna   win!   What   kind   of

Keep   on   train - ing   so   you're

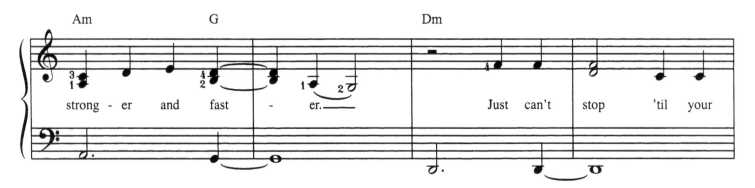

strong - er   and   fast   -   er.____   Just   can't   stop   'til   your

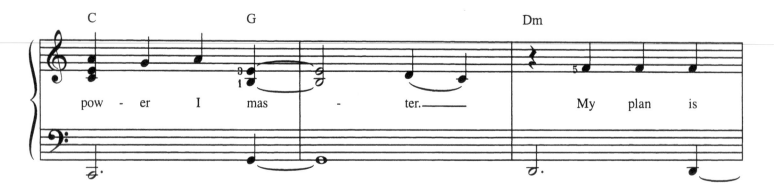

pow - er   I   mas   -   ter.____   My   plan   is

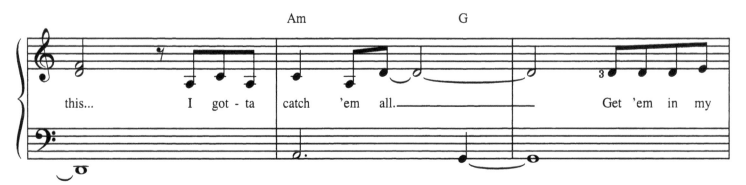

this...   I   got - ta   catch   'em   all.____   Get   'em   in   my

Po - ké - Ball.____ What kind of

D.S. al Coda II

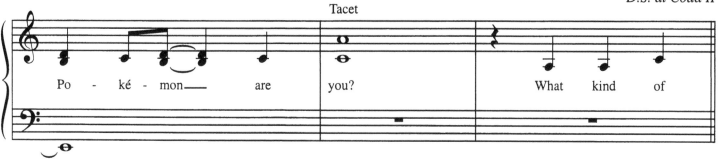

Po - ké - mon__ are you? What kind of

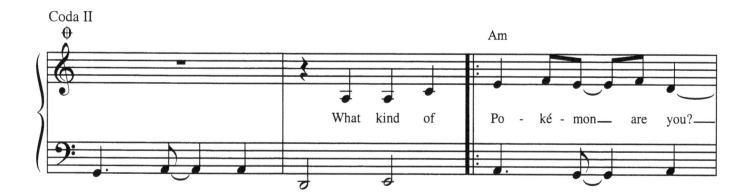

Coda II

__ How do you do the things__ you do?__ Po - ké - mon__ are you?__

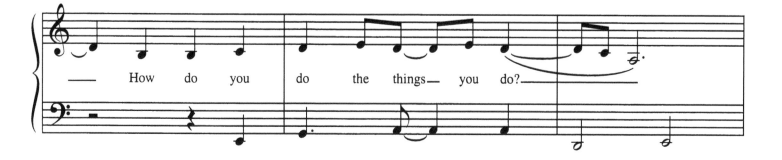

__ How do you do the things__ you do?__

Repeat and fade

What kind of

My Best Friends

Words and Music by
Michael Whalen

Moderately

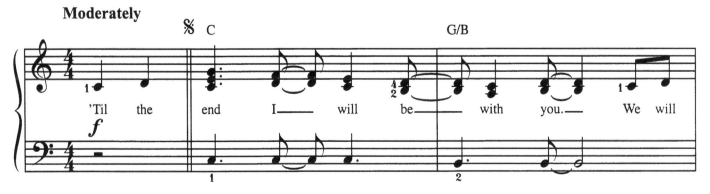

'Til the end I will be with you. We will

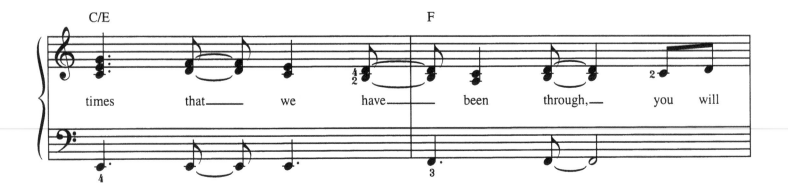

go where our dreams come true. All the

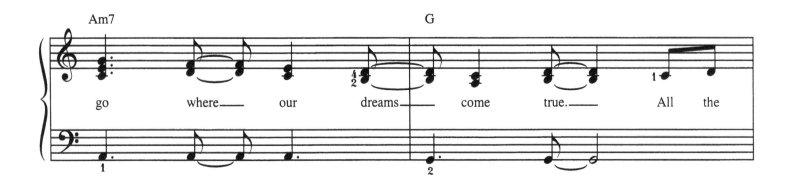

times that we have been through, you will

To Codas I and II

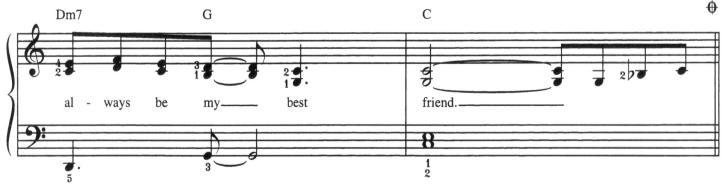

al-ways be my best friend.

Here we are on a new ad-ven-ture. Dan-ger lurks some-

where in the dark-ness. We are set for sur-pris-es, e-ven bat-tle!

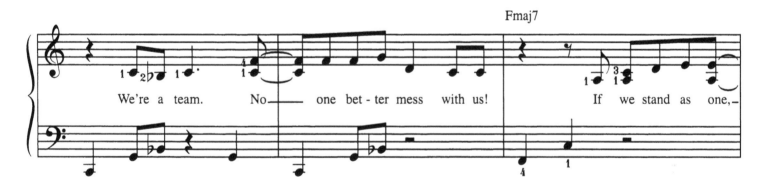

We're a team. No one bet-ter mess with us! If we stand as one,

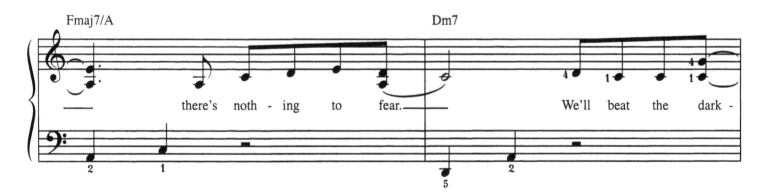

there's noth-ing to fear. We'll beat the dark-

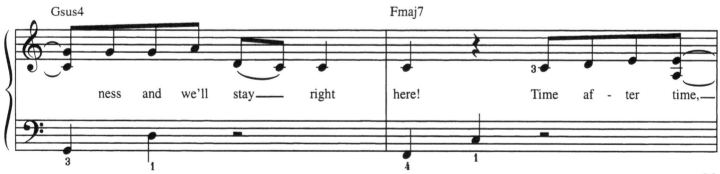

ness and we'll stay right here! Time af-ter time,

D.S. al Coda I

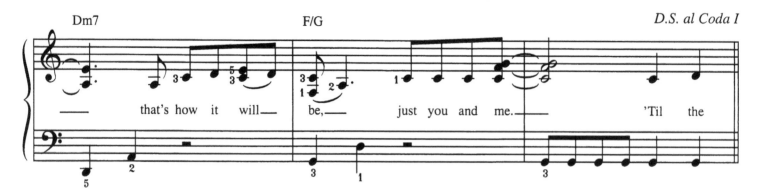

that's how it will— be,— just you and me.— 'Til the

Coda I

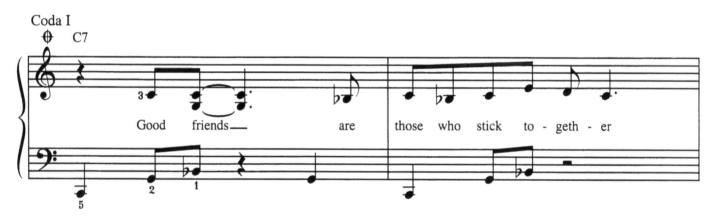

Good friends— are those who stick to - geth - er

when there's sun and in— the heav - y weath - er.—

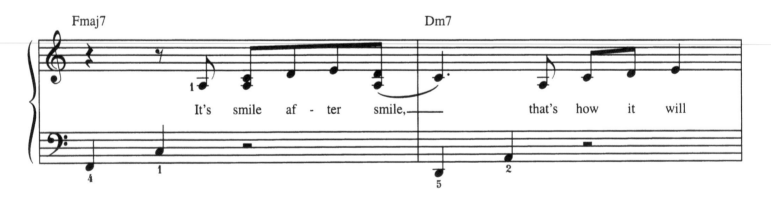

It's smile af - ter smile,— that's how it will

D.S. al Coda II

be,— just you and me.— 'Til the

Coda II

Re - mem - ber when we first met?

We had such fun, oh, I nev - er will for - get.

Since then, the times are so good. We've

D.S. and fade

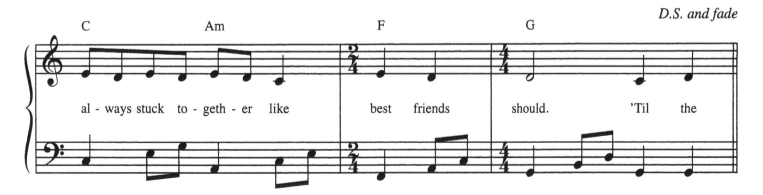

al - ways stuck to - geth - er like best friends should. 'Til the

Everything Changes

Words and Music by
T. Loeffler and Ken Cummings

Moderately fast

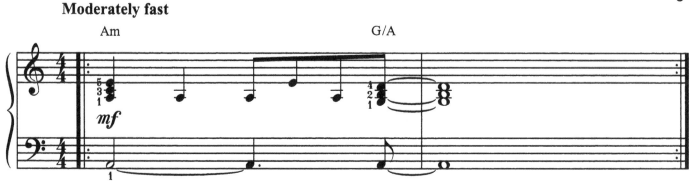

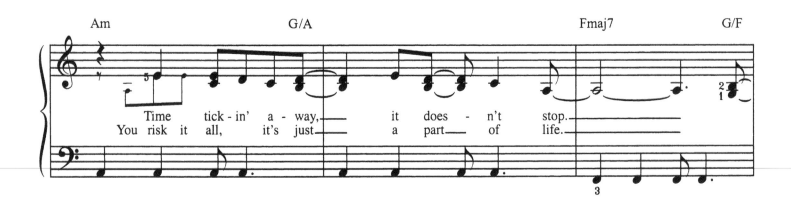

Your heart's beat - ing a - round the clock.
You take a chance, you throw the dice.

Time tick - in' a - way, — it does - n't stop.
You risk it all, it's just — a part — of life.

Ev - o - lu - tion is tak - ing place.
You hold on tight to what you know.

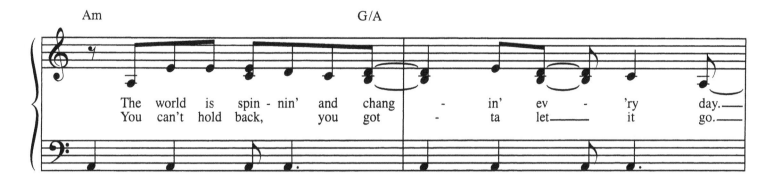

Am ... G/A

The world is spin - nin' and chang - in' ev - 'ry day.___
You can't hold back, you got - ta let___ it go.___

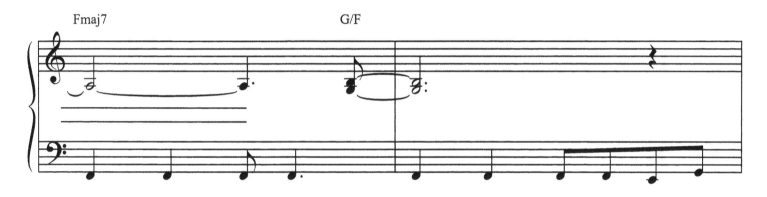

Fmaj7 ... G/F

Dm7

An - y - thing you think of with a name;___
Ev - 'ry lit - tle step of that you em - brace;___

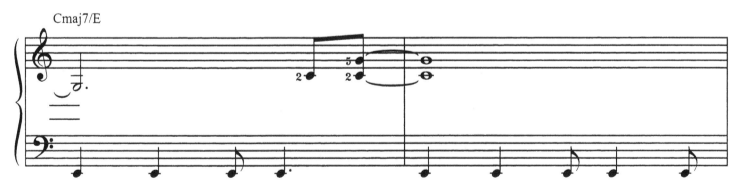

Cmaj7/E

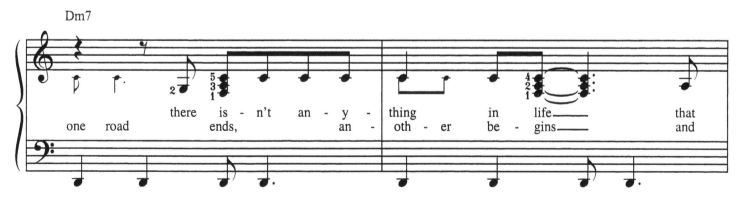

Dm7

there is - n't an - y - thing in life___ that
one road ends, an - oth - er be - gins___ and

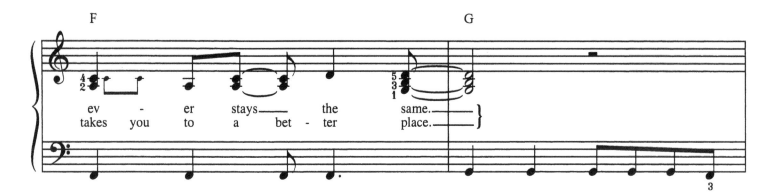

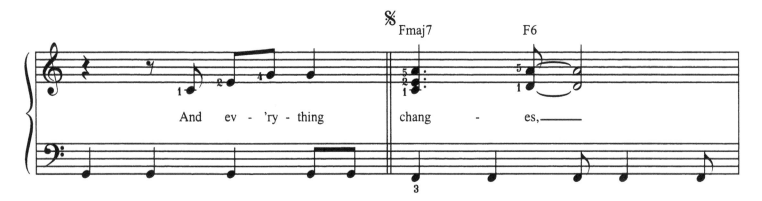

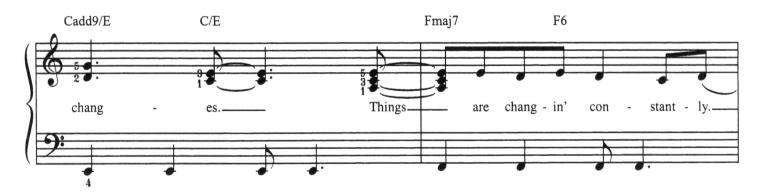

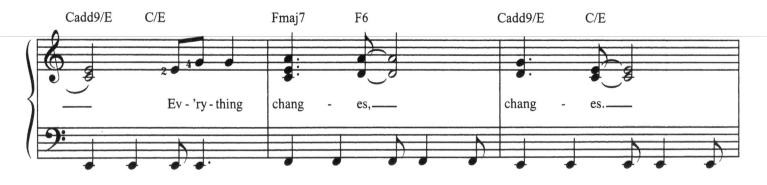

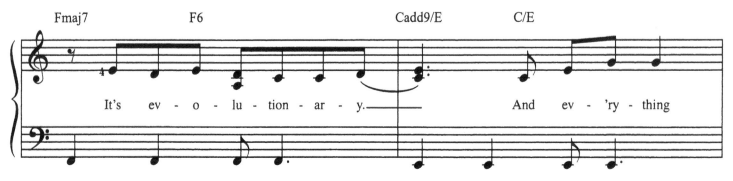

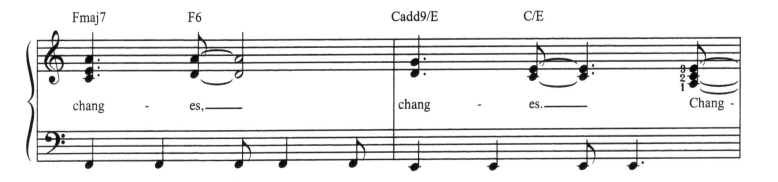

chang - es,_____ chang - es._____ Chang -

in' all the time, play - in' with your mind, mod -

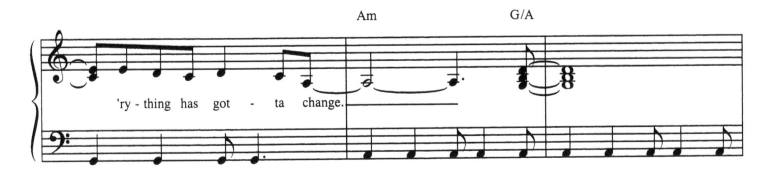

i - fied or re - ar - ranged._____ Ev -

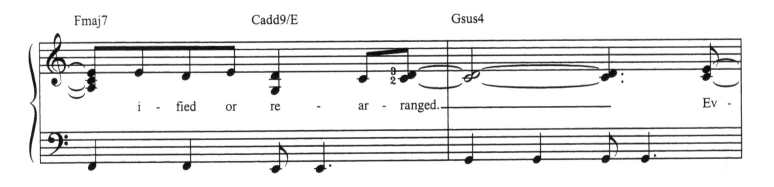

'ry - thing has got - ta change._____

And ev - 'ry - thing

The Time Has Come (Pikachu's Goodbye)

Words and Music by
T. Loeffler, J. Siegler,
and Norman Grossfeld

Moderately fast

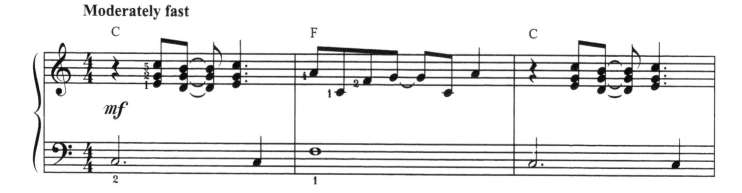

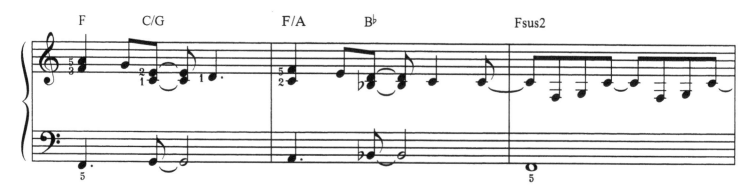

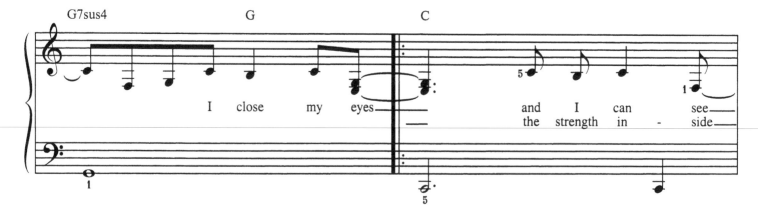

I close my eyes and I can see
the strength in - side

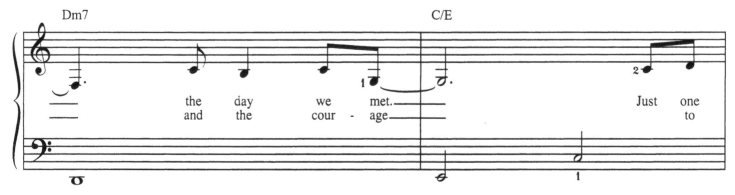

the day we met.
and the cour - age

Just one
to

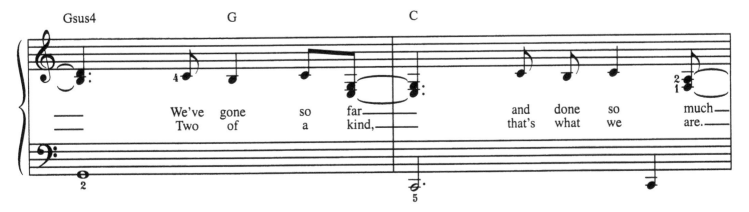

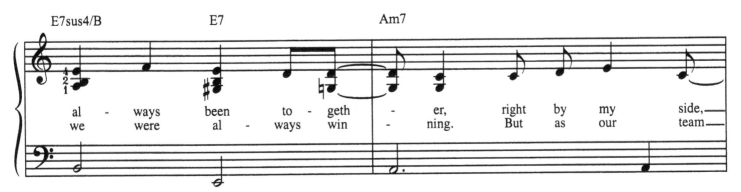

through thick and thin.___ You're the
is torn a - part,___ I

part of my life___ I'll al - ways re - mem - ber.___
wish we could go___ back to the be - gin - ning.___

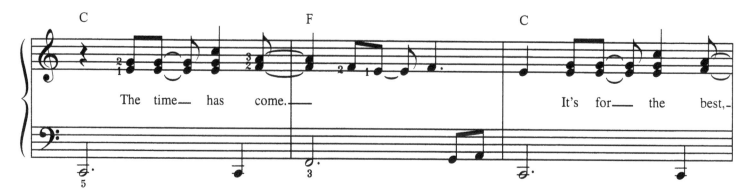

The time___ has come.___ It's for___ the best,___

___ I know___ it.___ Who could - 've guessed___ that you___ and I___

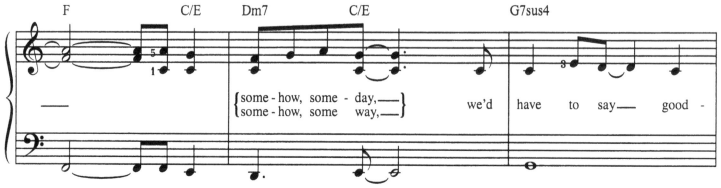

___ some - how, some - day,___ we'd have to say___ good -
some - how, some way,___

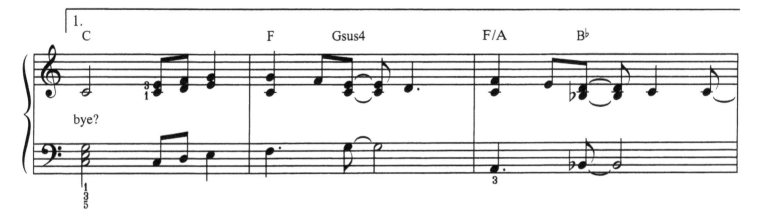

1.

C ... F Gsus4 F/A B♭

bye?

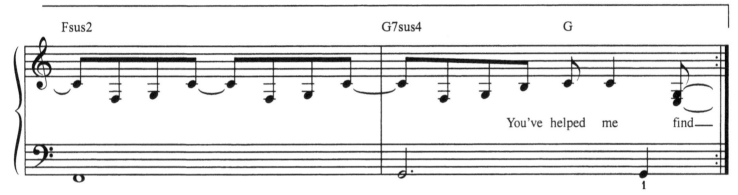

Fsus2 G7sus4 G

You've helped me find——

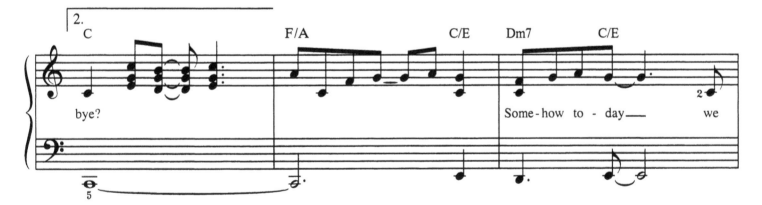

2.

C ... F/A C/E Dm7 C/E

bye? Some - how to - day—— we

F/G C F Gsus4

have to say—— good - bye.——

F/A B♭ Fsus2

Pokémon (Dance Mix)

Words and Music by
T. Loeffler and J. Siegler

Fast, with a driving beat

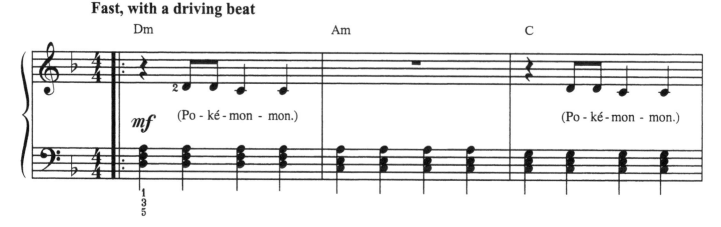

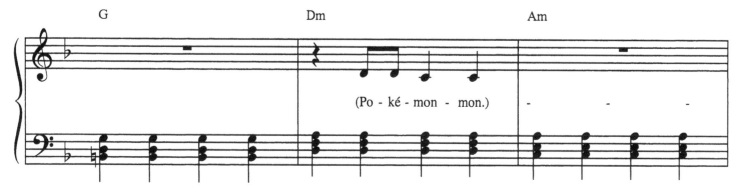

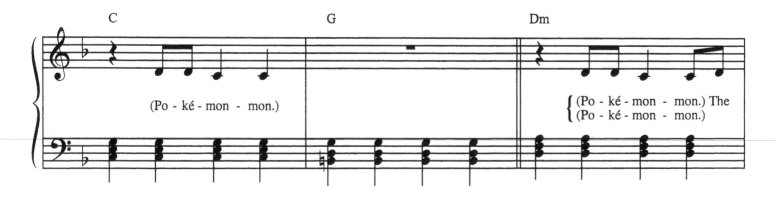

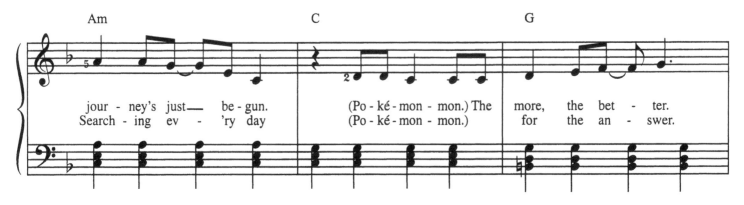

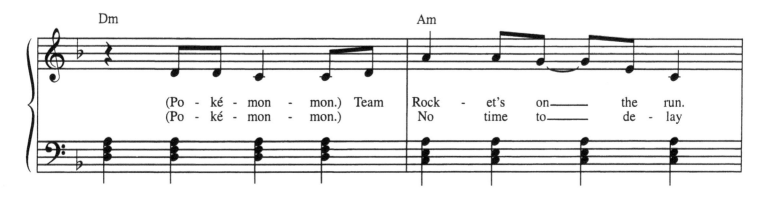

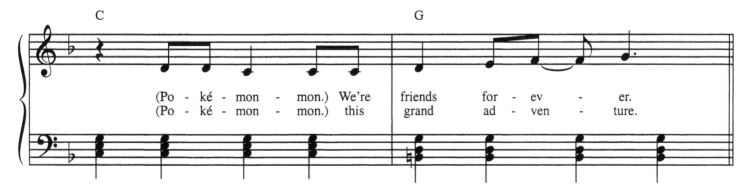

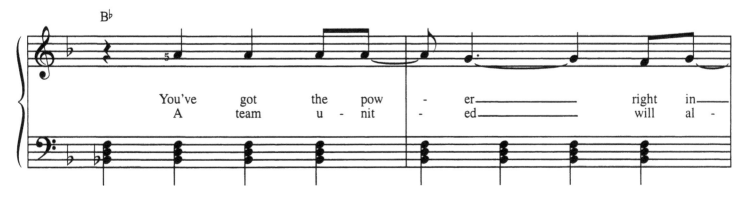

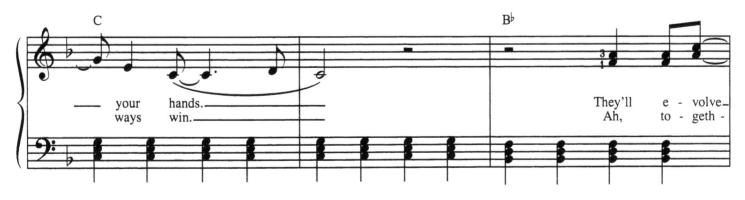

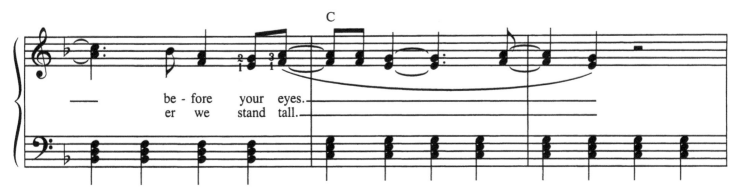

A world of mag - ic ___ at
Un - lock the se - crets ___

your com - mand. ___
deep with - in. ___

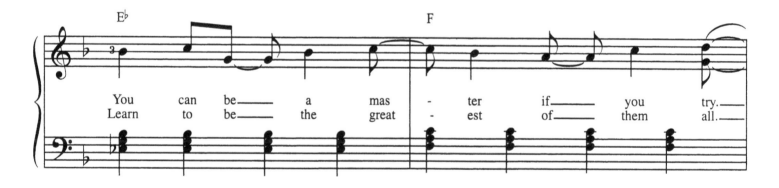

You can be ___ a mas - ter if ___ you try. ___
Learn to be ___ the great - est of ___ them all. ___

(Po - ké - mon - mon.)

Repeat and fade

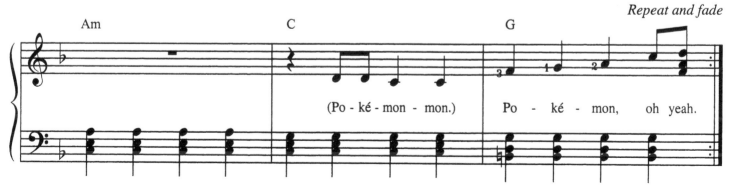

(Po - ké - mon - mon.)   Po - ké - mon,   oh yeah.

Double Trouble (Team Rocket)

Words and Music by
T. Loeffler, Bob Mayo
and Louis Cortelezzi

Moderately fast

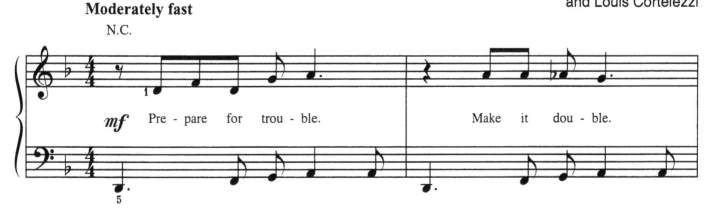

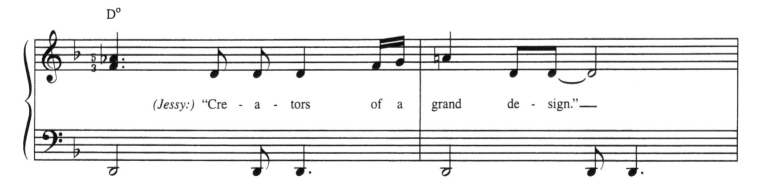

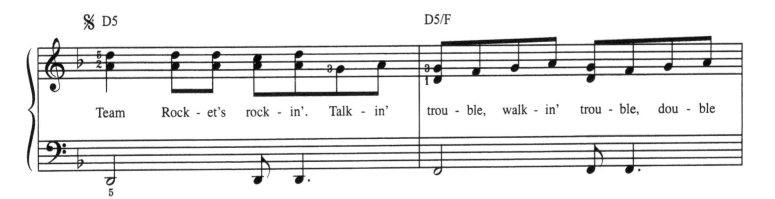

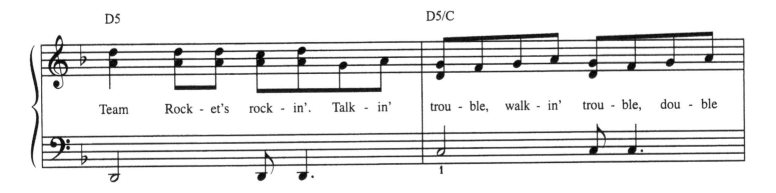

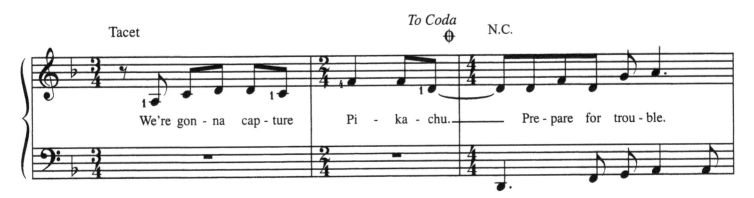

Make it dou - ble.

Prepare for trou - ble.

Dm

Make it dou - ble.

We're Team— Rock - et and we

D°

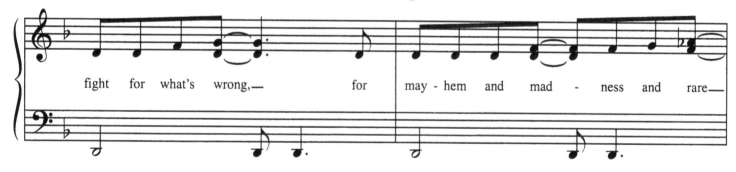

fight for what's wrong,— for may - hem and mad - ness and rare—

Gm/D

— Po - ké - mon.— (Jessy:) "I'm so gor - geous." (James:) "I'm

Dm   Tacet   *D.S. al Coda*

al - ways the man."   (The Boss:) "You're just the players in my master plan."

40

Coda

N.C.

We're al-

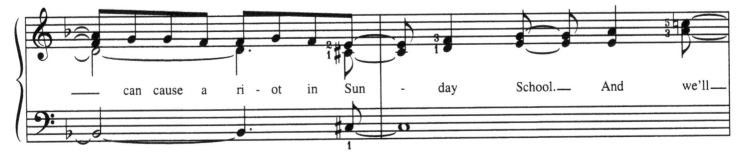

B♭maj7 C/B♭ B♭maj7

ways gon-na try it. No___ one can de-ny it. We___

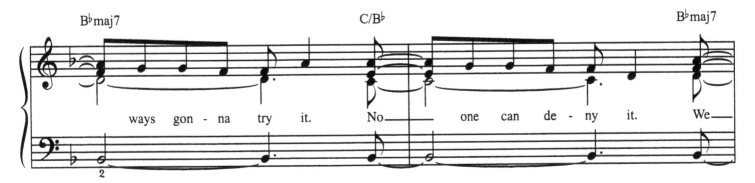

A/C#

___ can cause a ri-ot in Sun - day School.___ And we'll___

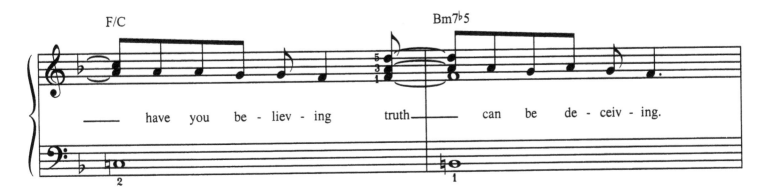

F/C Bm7♭5

___ have you be-liev-ing truth___ can be de-ceiv-ing.

Em7♭5 A7#9 N.C.

"Do un-to oth-ers" is our___ Gold-en Rule.___

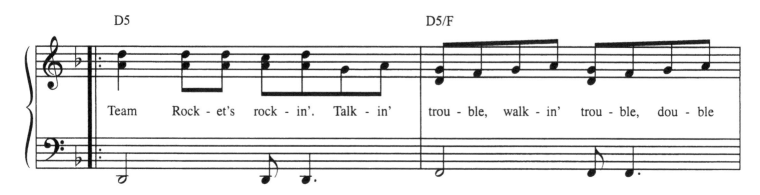

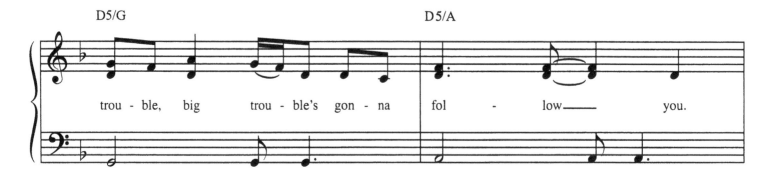

Together, Forever

Words and Music by
T. Loeffler and Ken Cummings

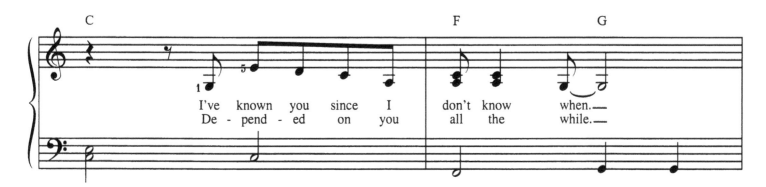

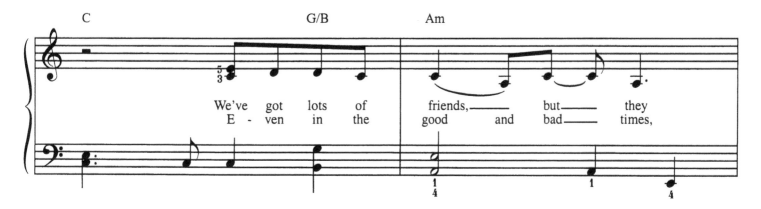

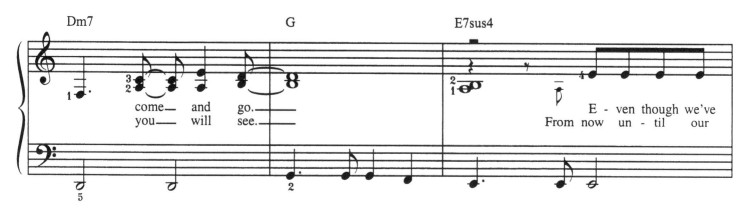

come and go._
you__ will see._

E - ven though we've
From now un - til our

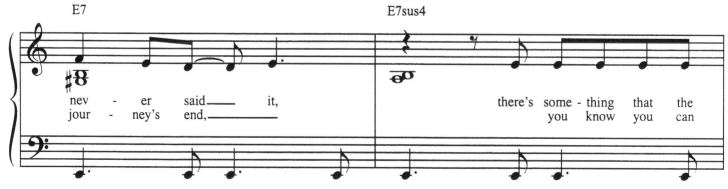

nev - er said__ it,
jour - ney's end,__

there's some - thing that the
you know you can

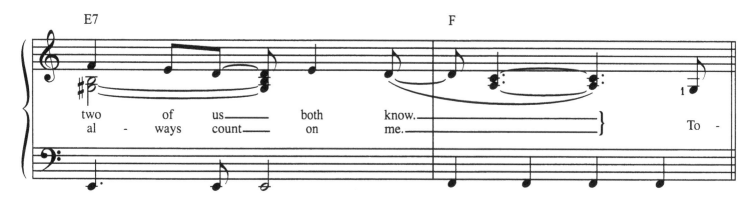

two of us__ both know._
al - ways count__ on me._

To -

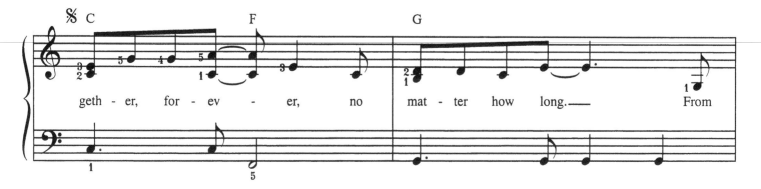

geth - er, for - ev - er, no
mat - ter how long.__ From

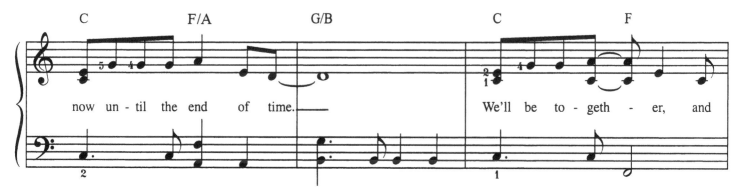

now un - til the end of time.__
We'll be to - geth - er, and

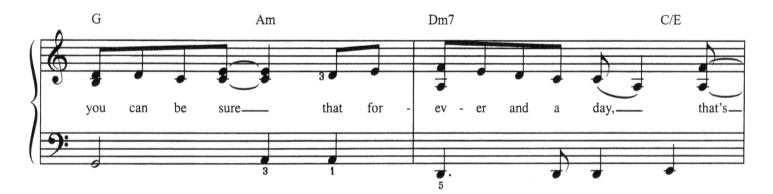

you can be sure___ that for - ev - er and a day,___ that's___

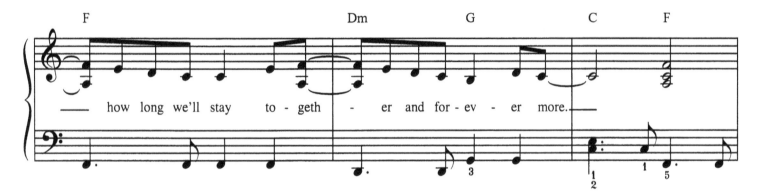

___ how long we'll stay to - geth - - er and for - ev - er more.___

No mat - ter where___ our des - ti - ny leads,___

___ I'll be there___ for___ you,___ al -

D.S. and fade

ways come through,___ and that you can___ be - lieve.___ To -

Misty's Song

Words and Music by
T. Loeffler and Ken Cummings

Slow Ballad

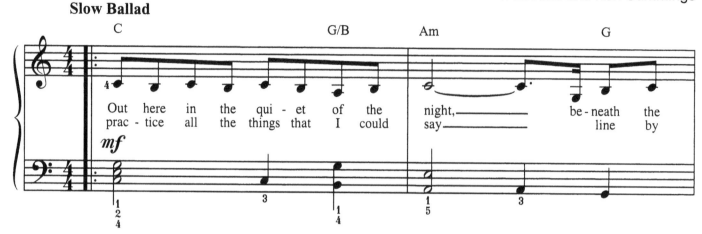

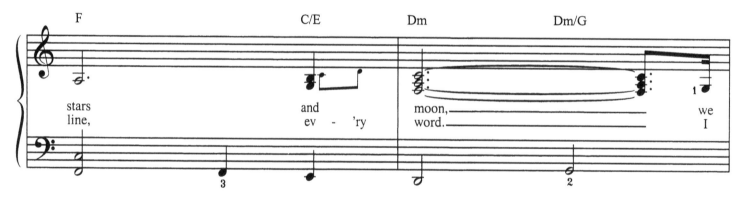

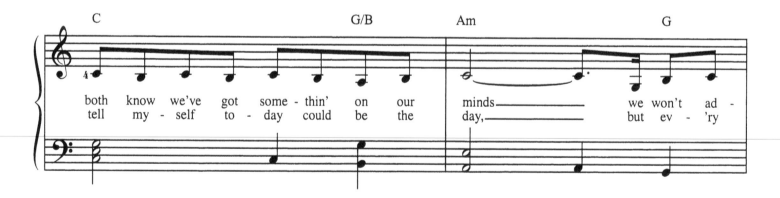

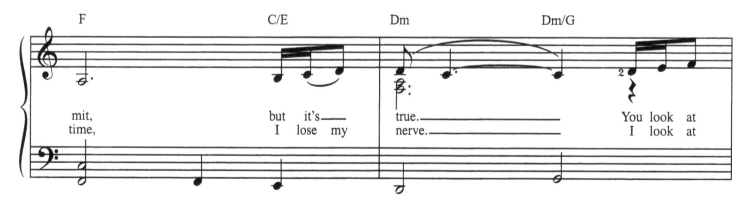

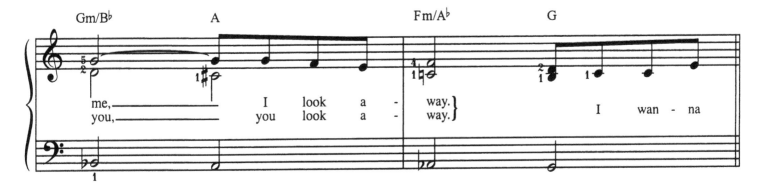

Gm/B♭ · A · Fm/A♭ · G

me,_____ I look a - way.
you,_____ you look a - way. } I wan - na

C · C+

tell you what I'm feel - ing, but I   don't know how to start. I wan - na

Dm · G7 · G/F

tell you, but now I'm a - fraid that   you might break my heart. Oh, why should

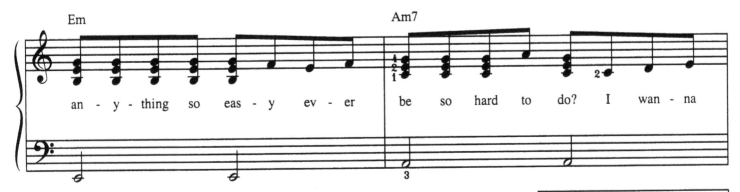

Em · Am7

an - y - thing so eas - y ev - er   be so hard to do? I wan - na

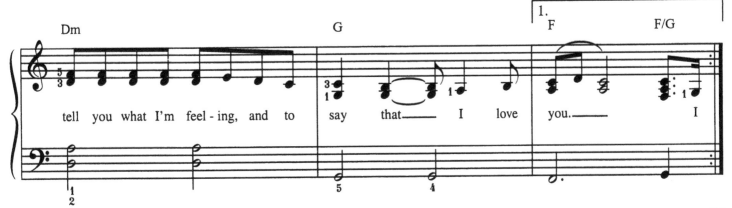

Dm · G · 1. F · F/G

tell you what I'm feel - ing, and to   say that____ I love you.____   I

2.

F   G   F

you.   Why,   why do you

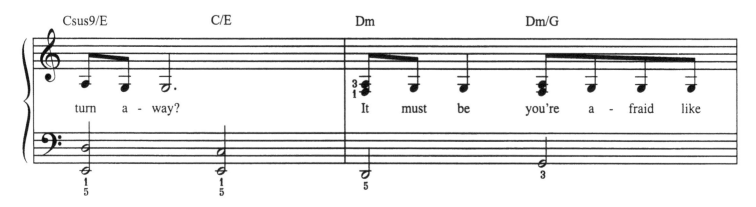

Csus9/E   C/E   Dm   Dm/G

turn a - way?   It must be you're a - fraid like

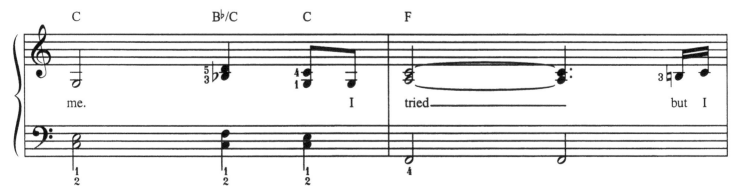

C   B♭/C   C   F

me.   I   tried————— but I

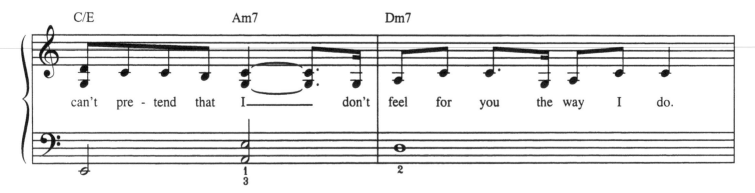

C/E   Am7   Dm7

can't pre - tend that I——— don't feel for you the way I do.

D.S. and fade

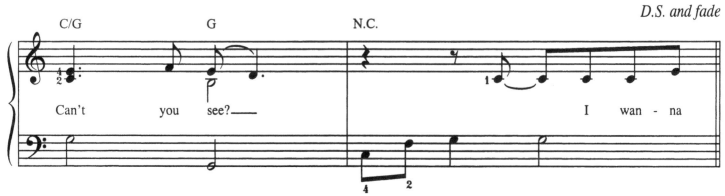

C/G   G   N.C.

Can't you see?——   I wan - na

PokéRAP

Words and Music by
T. Loeffler and J. Siegler

I want to be the best ___ there ev - er was. ___ To
cross the land, ___ look far and wide, ___ re -

beat all the rest, ___ yeah, ___ that's my ___ cause. ___ *(Spoken:)* *Electrode, Diglett, Nidoran, Mankey,*
lease from my hand _ the pow - er that's in - side. ___ *Venomoth, Poliwag, Nidorino, Golduck,*

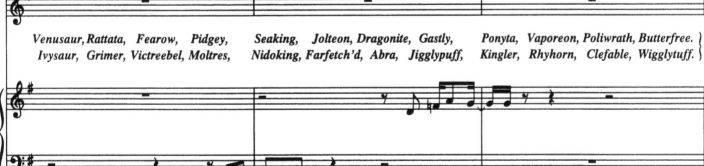

Venusaur, Rattata, Fearow, Pidgey, *Seaking, Jolteon, Dragonite, Gastly,* *Ponyta, Vaporeon, Poliwrath, Butterfree.*
Ivysaur, Grimer, Victreebel, Moltres, *Nidoking, Farfetch'd, Abra, Jigglypuff,* *Kingler, Rhyhorn, Clefable, Wigglytuff.*

Catch 'em, catch 'em. Got-ta catch 'em all! Po - ké - mon! I'll search a - Got-ta catch 'em all! Po - ké -

mon!

| Zubat, | Primeape, | Meowth, | Onix, | Geodude, Rapidash, | Magneton, | Snorlax, |
| Gengar, | Tangela, | Goldeen, | Spearow, | Weezing, Seel, | Gyarados, | Slowbro. |

Got-ta catch 'em all! Got-ta catch 'em all! Yeah. Got-ta catch 'em all! Got-ta catch 'em all! Yeah. Got-ta catch 'em all!_ Po - ké -

mon! Ow.

| Kabuto, Persian, | Paras, | Horsea, | Raticate, Magnemite, Kadabra, Weepinbell, |
| Ditto, Cloyster, | Caterpie, Sandshrew, | Bulbasaur, Charmander, Golem, Pikachu. |

%

F

C   **G**   **Am7**   **G/B**

At least one hun-dred and fif - ty or more _ to see. To be a Po-ké-mon Mas-ter is my

C   **D5**   **G5**

N.C.

des - ti - ny. _____

Alakazam, Doduo, Venonat, Machoke,   *Kangaskhan, Hypno, Electabuzz, Flareon,*
Charizard, Machamp, Pinsir, Koffing,   *Dugtrio, Golbat, Staryu, Magikarp,*

Tacet

Blastoise, Poliwhirl, Oddish, Drowzee, Raichu, Nidoqueen, Bellsprout, Starmie. "Whoo, we're at the half-way point,
Ninetales, Ekans, Omastar,   *Scyther, Tentacool, Dragonair, Magmar.* "Whoa, catch your breath, man. Shake out those

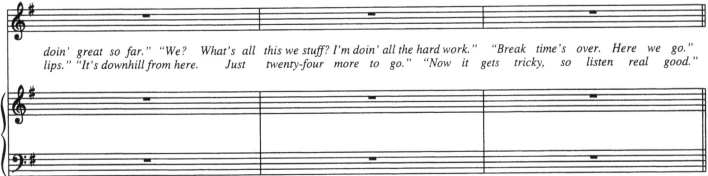

doin' great so far." "We? What's all this we stuff? I'm doin' all the hard work." "Break time's over. Here we go."
lips." "It's downhill from here.   Just   twenty-four more to go." "Now it gets tricky, so listen real good."

53

You Can Do It (If You Really Try)

Words and Music by
T. Loeffler, J. Siegler,
and Norman Grossfeld

Moderately fast

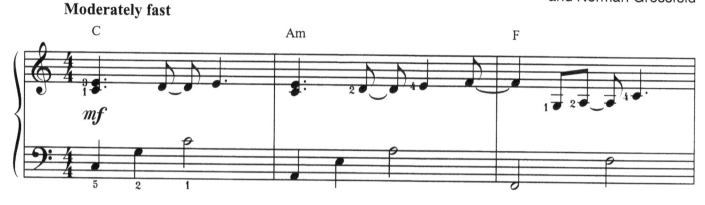

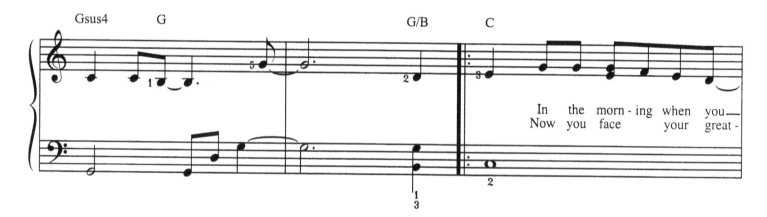

In the morn - ing when you___
Now you face your great -

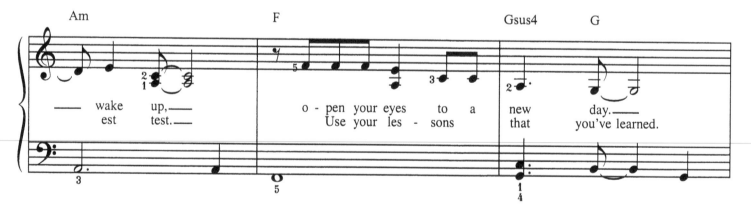

___ wake up,___
est test.___

o - pen your eyes to a new day.___
Use your les - sons that you've learned.

Look a - round at the gifts you've got.___
Your goal is to be the best___

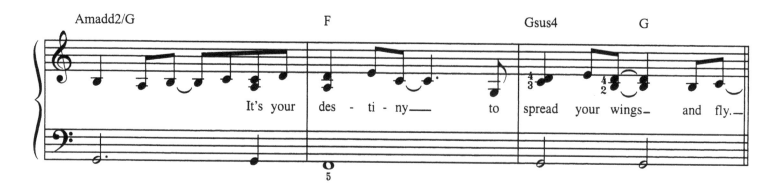

It's your des - ti - ny____ to spread your wings__ and fly.__

____ You can do it if you real - ly try.____ You can do it if you

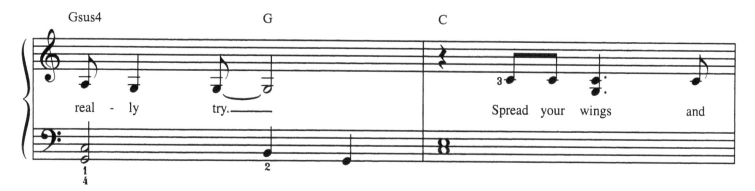

real - ly try.____ Spread your wings and

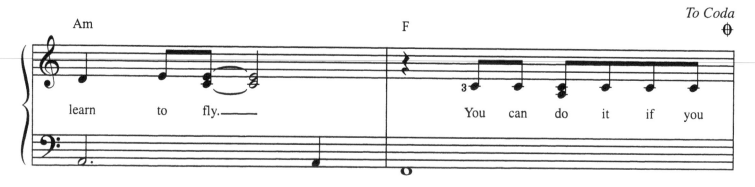

learn to fly.____ You can do it if you

D.S (take 2nd ending) al Coda

real - ly,____ real - ly try.__

Coda *D.S.S. and fade*

real - ly,____ real - ly try.__